Take Care Palagi
A Brief Grief Guidebook

Written and Illustrated by Erika Lei

Disclaimer

This book does not replace treatment for mental health conditions, nor is it a replacement for grief counseling. It's simply another avenue to try for children to move through their grieving process.

Take Care Palagi: A Brief Grief Guidebook
Written and Illustrated by Erika Lei
Edited by Taryn R. Wolf

Copyright © 2022 Erika Lei
All Rights Reserved

ISBN: 978-0-578-35118-6
Library of Congress Control Number: 2021925873

www.erikalei.com

For Mama Lani

If you're reading this right now, you just went through likely the most major life change you've ever gone through so far.

You're probably feeling the lowest and loneliest you've ever felt or think you're ever going to feel.

I'm *so* sorry this happened to you.

Losing a parent at a young age is something children should never have to experience.

I know reading this book won't fix everything, but I hope it'll help you find some peace.

I hope during your journey that this book helps you feel a little better than you did before.

This will take a long time. This is hard. There will be ups and downs, but you can make it through this.

Memories Worth Remembering

Right now, your head's filled with painful details of their passing; so, use the space in these next few pages to store your precious memories of them. Journal, draw, scribble some notes, write a poem —however you want to express yourself! These moments are how your parent want you to remember them—not sick in a hospital bed. This may be hard for you to do, but it's so important to help you heal. It's okay if you fill all these pages and need more space. It's okay if you don't. It's okay if you do it later.

Details of memories fade over time and I hope you come back to these good things when times get really tough.

Use all 5 senses (seeing, feeling, hearing, tasting, smelling) when describing your memory; this will keep it real.

What were your favorite things to do together?

What were some things you learned from them?

Describe your parent. What did they look like? Sound like? Smell like?

Dealing with the Hard Stuff

Immediately After

Please know this is the hardest part. You might not be able to eat, sleep, or even stop crying for a few days.

Your normal routine has been completely upended. This is going to be hard, but know you *can* make it, know you *will* make it.

Take it day by day. It's okay to cry.

Life isn't the same anymore. Life will never be the same again. You'll never be the same again. But, the you that you're creating is so amazing.

When days are really tough, focus on caring for yourself. Self-care can include: getting outside and sitting in the sun, playing, napping, taking a hot shower, cleaning your room, making art, reading, watching TV, etc.
What's something simple that makes you happy and you can add to your day?

Going Through Their Things

Being home after they die, regardless of whether they've been in the hospital or on hospice is so weird. It is. The things they used, created, wore…they all feel like items in a museum now. Walking around your home will be difficult at first. Each item may be tied to a memory. These items may make you feel like keeping them around will keep your parent alive.

Know these things are just things. The memories you have inside you are what have value. If the items have actual monetary value, you should probably keep them! Keep expensive items, photos, and then just a couple of other items that hold significant sentimental value. In the end, things are just things and you don't want to tie your parent to them.

Tips For Going Through Their Things

1. Make a game plan.
   - You can either split it up room-by-room, time frame for each session, who will participate in sorting with you, etc.
   - Be sure to check with people who aren't physically present if they want to keep anything.
   - Remember there's no right or wrong way.

2. Start with the least sentimental things.

3. Be prepared for strong emotions (it's okay to take a break or have something that brings you joy, like a friend, family member, or stuffed animal, to hug).

4. If you don't have a time limit, begin when you're ready. There's no set time frame for this.

5. Consider how much room you have to store things.

6. Think about if you're going to use it or wear it.
   - Don't feel guilty for getting rid of it; some of people's most cherished items were donated!

Not So Happy Holidays

There will be certain calendar dates that come around each year and you'll feel like no matter what you do, you can't avoid being reminded about their death. These days will be difficult immediately after, but it will get better as time goes by. If you're sad, it's okay to cry.

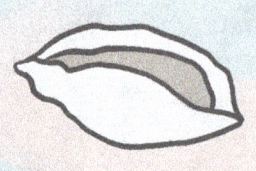
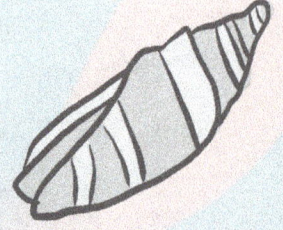

These dates are just days on a calendar. You can plan around them. Instead of spending them being sad, anxiously worrying about what could have been; why not try spending the day doing an activity that reminds you of them that you both loved? Eat your favorite foods that you shared. Walk in your favorite park that you frequented. Watch their favorite movies. Journal about them. These are positive ways to remember them and keep them alive.

Tips for Death Anniversary / Remembrance Day

It may help to make a plan of things to do for your parent's death anniversary. Here are some ideas:

- Tell stories about them with others.

- Look at photos and videos.

- Visit their gravesite and place flowers.

- Cook and eat their favorite meal.

- Listen to their favorite music.

- Write something to them.

- Go somewhere you feel close to them.

- Hold a moment of silence.

- Consider helping a charity that was close to their heart.

- Do something fun, like mini golf, reading, game night, video gaming, bowling, or roller skating.

Of course, you can always keep it simple and do nothing. Some years can be different from others. It's all up to you!

The Green Monster

As you grow older, you'll watch your friends go through life milestones and build relationships with their parents. You may feel like you're missing out or going through life alone, or you maybe even feel jealous of your peers. These feelings are completely normal.

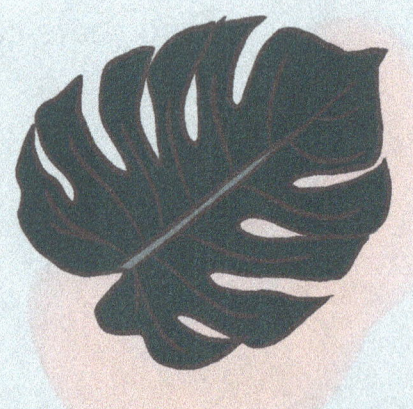

The idea of a "perfect family" is simply that—an idea. There's no such thing as a perfect family; what we may see on the surface as a perfect happy family may not be in the day-to-day. Everyone has ideals of what they want from their family relationships; it's normal to want close ones with your family. You'll build them again, be it with family members or not. You can choose who you call family.

Are You Projecting?

Trauma, like the death of a parent, can cause an unconscious reaction known as a "projection" where you blame others for your own issues. It's difficult to recognize in yourself.

Signs That You're Projecting:

- Feeling overly hurt or defensive about something someone did.
- You have difficulty standing in the other person's shoes.
- You feel strong emotions suddenly or have quick reactions.
- You have a headache, neck and shoulders are tense, jaw clenches, or some stomach issues.
- You say something that's only true for you, like saying "No one likes grapes", when only you don't.

What To Do:

1. The most important step is to recognize these cues in yourself. There's no reason to make someone else feel bad for something that isn't their fault.

2. Take a step back. If possible, physically separate yourself and take a moment to become you again.

3. Focus on your breathing. This will help to calm you down and gather your thoughts.

4. Be gentle and always forgive yourself. It'll take time to learn your triggers and respond in a way that you want to.

Truths to Remember

You'll never not be sad about this. Cry when you need to. In the beginning, it may seem like the tears are endless, but slowly with time, they'll fade. Certain calendar dates will bring tears for a while, but eventually you'll go long stretches without crying.

You never forget your parent or what happened, but you grow and learn to live with it. You no longer feel lonely because your life is full in ways you never thought were possible. Sometimes (rarely) you'll find yourself brought to tears, triggered by certain events, but these just serve as reminders of the love you shared. We miss what we love and felt love from—it's normal and human to cry about it.

It does get better with time—believe this. However, there's no time-frame. Take your time. Everything in this book will probably be hard immediately after your parent passes. They'll take time to go through. You may go through cycles of feeling good and feeling like you're making it through, then you slide back and feel the sadness wash over you again.

This is normal and it's okay. Remember whenever you are in these fits of sadness that these are temporary feelings; you'll make it out of it, and you'll be okay. You are not alone—don't forget about all of your friends and family who love you. It was hard to lose your parent, but remember they miss them, too. Support each other.

No one will ever replace them. You may seek mentors or even parent-type figures throughout your life, but know that no one can ever truly replace what you had with your parent. It's unfair for you to place those expectations on new relationships.
If you had a single parent, and they're now gone, this is so hard and scary. Remember, your caregivers do want what's best for you. They're trying their best. Give them grace. They're probably just as scared about the new situation as you. If you feel at all unsafe though, please let someone in charge at your school, church, foster care, or other place you go often, know.

Because you lost your parent early in life, all you have now are ideas of what a parent should be. Nobody's perfect. It's unrealistic to think that someone or even your parent who died could be that person in your head. Don't try to replace your parent. The relationships you have in your life are each special in their own ways.

There's nothing wrong with you. You did nothing to "deserve" this. This didn't happen to you because you were "bad." You're grieving because you loved and were loved.

You're capable of so much more love in the future. You'll be surrounded by more love than you ever thought possible. It starts with loving yourself. You're so strong and you're so lovable. You now have a deep, early understanding of life and compassion—and people will love learning about you and your soul because of it.

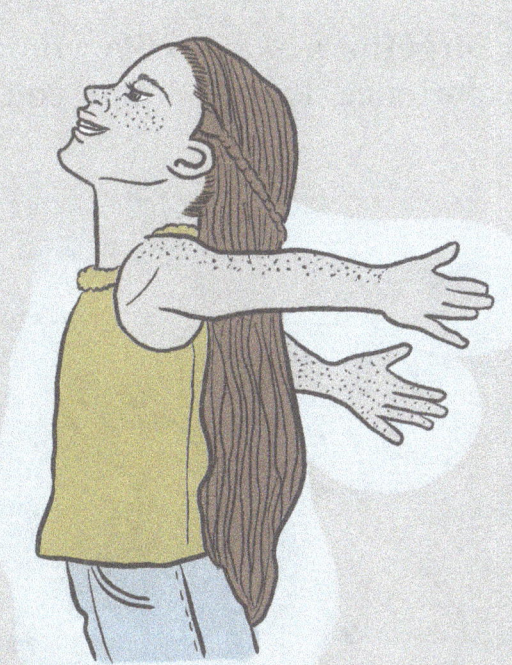
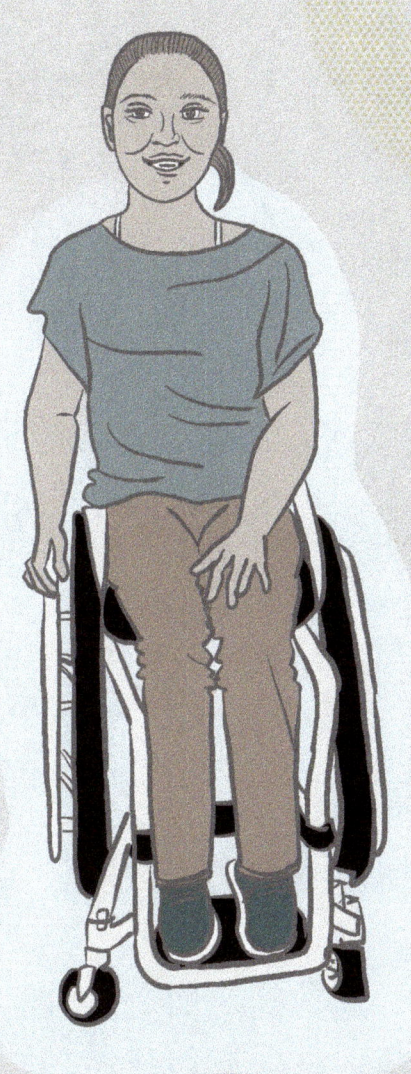

Don't ever forget: it's okay to live your life.
This experience doesn't define you.

Some days, it may feel like you may never recover from this or even get out of bed, but you will make it through this. You will continue to live your life and you will accomplish so much.

Sometimes you may feel: "I wish my parent were here to see this" or want some validation that you'll truly never get. It's normal to want this, but the most important validation you'll ever receive is from yourself. Always stay true to yourself and believe in yourself. You have the power within you and this is all your parent ever wanted for you.

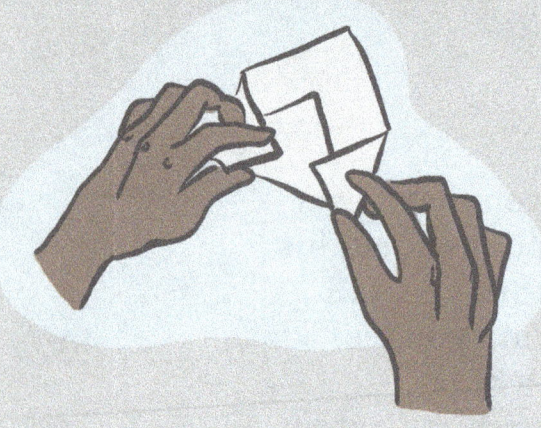
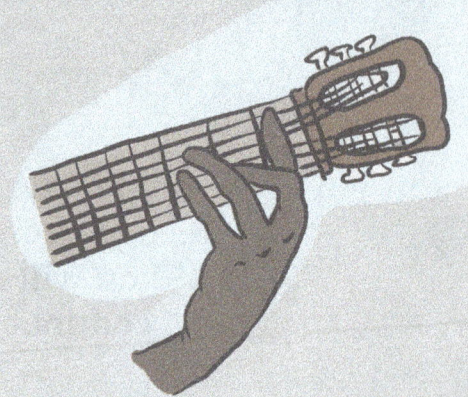

Life is hard. Life is unfair. Life is too short. But, life is also beautiful and full of so many moments that make it worth it. There are so many more good things to come in your life. There are so many more dogs to pet, places to see, ice creams to try, and people to love you!

As you continue on your journey, you'll find you'll use less energy being sad, anxious, and worrying. Instead, you'll find yourself using your energy to create, trust, and grow.

Keep believing in yourself; your life is just beginning.

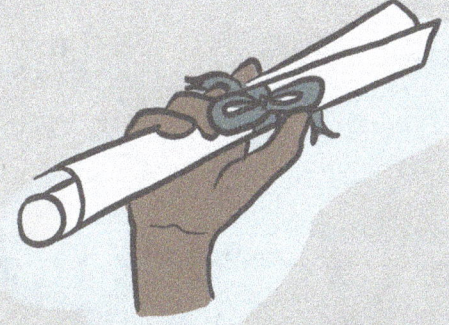

Affirmations To Say Out Loud

Say these as much as you want to!

1. I can overcome hard things.//
2. I am in control of my emotions.//
3. I believe in myself.//
4. I am going after my dreams.//
5. I make the world a better place.//
6. It gets better with time.//
7. I'm capable and worthy of love.//
8. It's okay to live my life.//
9. I use my energy to create, trust, and grow.//
10. My life is just beginning.

Additional Resources

Grief is a natural response to loss. However, how we process this grief differs from person to person. Here are some additional resources to consider as a young person in this journey to healing:

Comfort Zone Camp: free camps held year-round in locations across the United States are available for children 7-17 who have suffered the loss of a parent, sibling or primary caregiver
http://www.comfortzonecamp.org/

The Dougy Center: variety of grief resources including physical locations for children and families experiencing grief
https://www.dougy.org/

National Alliance for Grieving Children: online education and extensive database to assist children and teens throughout the grieving process
https://childrengrieve.org

www.ingramcontent.com/pod-product-compliance
Lightning Source LLC
Chambersburg PA
CBHW062108160426
42813CB00100B/1179